Table of Contents

Introduction

Compendia of instructions for the preparation of Jewish food or addressed to the Jewish reader constitute the single largest body of literature written by and for Jewish women. These cookbooks initially arose during the first half of the nineteenth century in response to the social aspirations of those who wished to add culinary refinement to the kosher kitchen. Among the earliest extant examples are several small Yiddish manuscripts from Bohemia, Moravia, or neighboring areas; they were in all likelihood intended to teach young brides to cook or to supervise a servant in the kitchen. Jewish women continued to learn to cook from one another and to write manuscript cookbooks, even after printed ones specifically addressed to them made their appearance during the early 1800s. Most Jewish cookbooks in the nineteenth century were written in German, the most popular being Rebekka Wolf's Kochbuch für israelitische Frauen: Enthaltend die verschiedensten Koch- und Backarten, mit einer vollständigen Speisekarte so wie einer genauen Anweisung zur Einrichtung und Führung einer religiös-jüdischen Haushaltung, which appeared in Berlin in 1856: it went through 14 editions, stayed in print for almost 80 years, and was the basis for the first extant cookbook published in Yiddish Oyzer Bloshteyn's Kokhbuch far yudishe froyen, which appeared in Vilna in 1896 and New York in 1898. Wolf's cookbook was also translated into Polish, as Kuchnia Koszerna (1904), and other languages. As was common, Bloshteyn (known also as Auser Blaustein, 1840–1898) lifted recipes from other authors, above all Wolf, and even imitated her decorative covers. Bloshteyn promised young women and cooks 668 economical and tasty recipes for preparing a wide variety of dishes, including Jewish specialties, "collected from various famous cookbooks in various languages," but adapted to the Jewish kitchen and suitable for everyday cooking as well as for catering weddings. Bloshteyn, a writer of romantic novels and a translator who also published dictionaries and grammars of Russian, Yiddish, and Hebrew, offered several scenarios in which his cookbook would save the day: the elegant young woman who was too busy studying, sewing, and knitting to learn how to cook or how to instruct her servant properly; the inexperienced servant, who needed guidance; and the experienced housewife searching for new and unusual delicacies. While educated readers could of course read cookbooks in other languages, he explained, those books did not address the specific needs of the Jewish reader, though in fact many did, including the one from which he himself purloined. By the last decades of the nineteenth century, East European Jewish cookbooks were appearing in Russian, Hungarian, and other languages.Most of the authors were women. Marie Kauders was a widow with more than 40 years experience when she published her award-winning Erstes israelitisches Kochbuch für böhmische Küche in 1886. She also published a cookbook for her Jewish cooking school in Prague, which trained cooks for Jewish restaurants and wedding catering. Kauders insisted that cooking was an art on a par with sculpture. Such volumes reflected not only Jewish social aspirations, but also new domestic challenges: there were newfangled stoves and novel products such as solid vegetable fats. As these items were kosher and pareve, they could replace animal fats and offer greater flexibility to the kosher cook, but women needed instruction in how to use them. Sparsames koscheres Kochen, which appeared in the 1930s, promoted Ceres cooking fat, a hydrogenated coconut oil, and Omega margarine, products of the Schicht company of Schreckenstein (now Strekov, Czech Republic).

Prior to 1900

By the first half of the 19th-century, a few Jewish manuscript cookbooks appear in Yiddish (Bohemia, Moravia, or neighboring areas); German ones appear in greater numbers throughout the century; and by the 1890s, there are Osmanli ones from Salonika. The first known published volume is J. Stolz's Kochbuch der Israeliten, oder prakt. Unweisung, wie man nach dem juedischen Religionsgruenden alle Gattungen der feinsten Speisen kauscher bereitet (Carlsruhe, 1815). During the 19th century, over a dozen Jewish cookbooks were published in German, more than in any other language. The most successful, Kochbuch fuer Israelitische Frauen: Ent haltend die verschiedensten Koch- und Backarten, mit einer vollständigen Speisekarte so wie einer genauen Anweisung zur Einrichtung und Fuehrung einer religioes-juedischen Haushaltung (Berlin, 1856) by Rebekka Wolf (née Heinemann), went through 14 editions. In print for almost 80 years, it was translated into Dutch (1881) and Polish

(1904), and influenced the first known cookbook published in Yiddish, Ozer Bloshsteyn's Kokhbuch far yudishe [sic] froyen (Vilna, 1896; New York, 1898). These kosher cookbooks, which emphasized fine cuisine and gracious living, were part of a larger adaptation of mainstream bourgeois domestic values within an acculturating modern Orthodox community. The first published English cookbook, The Jewish Manual, or Practical Information in Jewish and Modern Cookery: With a Collection of Valuable Recipes & Hints Relating to the Toilette (London, 1846), by "A Lady," aimed to refine the kosher table, but with an English and Western Sephardi emphasis. The anonymous author was recently identified as Judith Lady. Montefiore, who dedicated some of her philanthropic energies to educating Jewish girls for domestic service by establishing cookery classes at a Jewish orphanage and school. This book appeared in a single edition, although parts of it were reprinted, without attribution, in 1864 and 1867 in Australia. By the last decade of the 19th century, kosher gourmet cookbooks also appeared in Dutch, Hungarian, Russian, and Italian, and the German volumes were becoming larger and more elaborately bound. The grandest, Marie Elsasser's Ausfuehrliches Kochbuch fuer die einfache und feine juedische Kueche unter Beruecksichtigung aller rituellen Vorschriften in 3759 Rezepten (Frankfurt, 1901), was over 900 pages. The custom of giving cookbooks to brides accounts in part for the lavishness of such volumes.

Recipe

Bazargan

- 1/3 cup (30 g) walnut halves, roughly chopped

- 1/4 cup (30 g) pine nuts

- 1 1/4 cups (200 g) fine or medium bulgur

- 2 1/2 cups (590 ml/20 fl oz) boiling water

- 2 medium shallots, finely chopped

- 1 medium bunch flat-leaf parsley, stems trimmed and finely chopped

- 3 tablespoons tamarind paste or pomegranate molasses

- 1 tablespoon tomato paste (purée)

- 2 tablespoons honey

- 1 tablespoon fresh lemon juice

- 3 tablespoons extra-virgin olive oil

- 1 teaspoon ground cumin

- 1/2 teaspoon Aleppo pepper flakes

- 1/2 teaspoon dried mint

- 1 teaspoon kosher salt, or more to taste

Directions

- In a small frying pan, toast the walnuts and pine nuts over medium-low heat, shaking pan occasionally, until fragrant and lightly browned, 5–7 minutes. Immediately transfer the nuts to a bowl and let cool.

- Combine the bulgur and the boiling water in a heatproof medium bowl and let sit until bulgur is tender but still slightly chewy, about 30 minutes. Drain well and transfer to a large bowl along with the shallots, parsley, and toasted walnuts and pine nuts.

- In a medium bowl, whisk together the tamarind paste, tomato paste (purée), honey, lemon juice, olive oil, cumin,

Aleppo pepper, mint, salt, and black pepper. Drizzle the dressing over the bulgur mixture and toss to combine.

• Taste and add more salt, if desired. Transfer to a serving bowl and sprinkle generously with pomegranate seeds.

Tabbouleh

Ingredients

• 3⁄4 cup (125 g) fine or medium bulgur

• 2 cups (475 ml/16 fl oz) boiling water

• 1 1⁄2 lb (680 g) tomatoes (3–4 medium), seeded and finely chopped

• 2 Persian (mini) cucumbers, finely chopped

• 1 cup (50 g) finely chopped fresh flat-leaf parsley

• 1 cup (50 g) finely chopped fresh mint or cilantro, (coriander), from 1 large bunch

• 1 small bunch scallions (spring onions), white and green parts, thinly sliced

• Finely grated zest of 1 lemon

• 1⁄4 cup (60 ml) fresh lemon juice

- 1/4 cup (60 ml) extra-virgin olive oil

- 1 1/2 teaspoons kosher salt

- 1/2 teaspoon freshly ground black pepper

Directions

- Combine the bulgur and the boiling water in a heatproof bowl and let sit until the bulgur is tender but still slightly chewy, about 30 minutes. Drain well and transfer to a large bowl along with the tomatoes, cucumbers, parsley, mint, and scallions (spring onions).

- In a small bowl, whisk together the lemon zest, lemon juice, olive oil, salt, and pepper Add to the bulgur bowl and toss to combine. Serve immediately.

Hummus With Spiced Meat

Ingredients

- 2 tablespoons extra-virgin olive oil, plus more for drizzling

- 1 large onion, finely chopped

- 4 garlic cloves, finely chopped

- 1/4 cup (30 g) pine nuts

- 1 teaspoon ground cumin

- 1/2 teaspoon ground cinnamon

- 1/2 teaspoon smoked paprika

- 1/2 teaspoon ground turmeric

- 1/2 teaspoon kosher salt, or more to taste

- 1/4 teaspoon freshly ground black pepper

- 1 lb (455 g) ground (minced) beef

- 1 teaspoon Harissa

Directions

- In a large frying pan, heat the oil over medium heat. Add the onion and cook, stirring occasionally, until softened and lightly browned, 6–8 minutes.

- Add the garlic, pine nuts, cumin, cinnamon, smoked paprika, turmeric, salt, and pepper and stir until fragrant, about 1 minute.

- Add the ground (minced) beef and cook, breaking up the meat into small pieces with a spoon, until just cooked through, 4–5 minutes.

• Remove the pan from the heat and stir in the harissa.Spoon the hummus onto a large serving plate and make a wide, shallow well in it with the back of a spoon.

• Mound the spiced beef into the well, then top with a generous sprinkle of za'atar and parsley, and a drizzle of additional olive oil

Caponata Alla Giudia
Ingredients

• ¼ cup (30 g) pine nuts

• Extra-virgin olive oil, for frying

• 1½ lb (680 g) eggplant (aubergine), peeled and cut into

• ½-inch (1.25 cm) pieces

• 1 large yellow onion, finely chopped

• 2 celery stalks, finely chopped

• 3 large garlic cloves, minced or pushed through a press

• Kosher salt and freshly ground black pepper

• 3/4 lb (340 g) tomatoes, peeled, seeded, and finely chopped

* 3 tablespoons apple cider vinegar

* 1 tablespoon sugar

* 2 tablespoons brine-packed capers, drained

* 1/3 cup (45 g) finely chopped pitted green olives

* ¼ cup (35 g) golden raisins (sultanas)

* Chopped fresh parsley, for garnish

Directions

* In a small dry frying pan, toast the pine nuts to over medium-low heat, shaking the pan occasionally, until fragrant and lightly browned, about 5 minutes. Transfer the pine nuts to a bowl to cool.

* In a large frying pan, heat about ¼ inch (6 mm) olive oil over medium heat until shimmering. Add the eggplant (aubergine) pieces and cook, turning occasionally, until golden brown and softened but not mushy, about 10 minutes. Transfer the eggplant to a large bowl. If the pan looks dry, add another tablespoon of oil.

* Add the onion, celery, garlic, and a generous pinch of salt and cook, stirring occasionally, until crisp-tender, about 5

minutes. Add the tomatoes, vinegar, sugar, capers, olives, golden raisins, 11/4 teaspoons salt, and a generous amount of black pepper.Cook, stirring occasionally, until the tomatoes soften, 6–8 minutes. Stir in the fried eggplant (with any residual oil from cooking) and pine nuts, cook until the mixture thickens slightly, about 5 minutes.

• Remove from the heat and transfer to a serving bowl. Let stand for at least 30 minutes before serving to allow the flavors to meld. Taste and adjust salt, if desired.

Chremslach
Ingredients

• 3 sheets matzo

• ½ cup (70 g) raisins

• ¼ cup (35 g) whole almonds, finely chopped

• 3 eggs

• 1/3 cup (40 g) matzo meal

• 1/3 cup (65 g) sugar, plus more for serving

• 1 teaspoon ground cinnamon

• 1 teaspoon finely grated lemon zest

- 1 tablespoon fresh lemon juice

- ¼ teaspoon kosher salt

- Vegetable oil, for frying

- Honey, for serving

Directions

- Add the matzo sheets to a small baking dish and cover with warm water. Soak for 10 minutes then squeeze completely dry and place in a medium bowl. Add the raisins, almonds, eggs, matzo meal, sugar, cinnamon, lemon zest, lemon juice, and salt and mix well to combine.

- In a large frying pan, heat ¼ inch (6 mm) vegetable oil over medium heat. Line a large plate with a few layers of paper towel. Working in batches of 5–6, spoon the batter by the rounded tablespoonful into the oil, pressing down gently with the back of the spoon to flatten.

- Fry, turning once, until golden brown on both sides, 3–4 minutes.

• Transfer the fritters to the paper towels to drain. Serve warm or at room temperature drizzled with honey or dusted with sugar.

Ingredients

For the filling:

• 2 tablespoons vegetable oil

• 1 small onion, finely chopped

• Kosher salt and freshly ground black pepper

• 10 oz (285 g) thawed frozen spinach, squeezed dry and roughly chopped

• 1 egg, lightly beaten

• 1 garlic clove, minced or pushed through a press

• ½ teaspoon dried dill

• ½ cup (120 g) ricotta cheese

• 4 oz (115 g) feta cheese, crumbled

For assembly and baking:

• Flour, for dusting

• 2 sheets frozen puff pastry, thawed

• Egg wash: 1 egg beaten with 1 teaspoon water

• Sesame seeds, for sprinkling

Make the filling:

• In a small frying pan, heat the oil over medium heat.

• Add the onion and a pinch of salt and cook, stirring occasionally, until softened and lightly browned, 6–8 minutes. Remove from the heat and let cool.

• Transfer the cooked onion to a bowl and add the spinach, egg, garlic, dill, ricotta, feta, ¼ teaspoon salt, and ¼ teaspoon pepper and mix well.

Assemble and bake the turnovers:

• Preheat the oven to 350°F (180°C/Gas Mark 4). Line two large baking sheets with parchment paper.

• On a lightly floured surface, gently roll out 1 sheet of puff pastry into a 12-inch (30 cm) square, trimming any ragged edges. Cut the square of pastry into nine 4-inch (10 cm) squares. Spoon about 2 tablespoons of the spinach filling near one corner of each square and use your fingers or the back of a spoon to lightly flatten. Fold the opposite corner over to meet it, making a triangle and locking the filling inside. Press firmly all along the edges to seal, lightly wetting fingers with water, if necessary. Repeat with the second sheet of puff pastry and remaining filling.

• Lay the filled bourekas on the baking sheets. Brush the tops with the egg wash (you may not use all of it) and sprinkle with sesame seeds. Bake until puffed and golden brown, 30–35 minutes. Set the baking sheets on wire racks to cool. Serve warm or at room temperature

Wine-Braised Pot Roast

Ingredients

• 3–4 lb (1.35–1.8 kg) boneless beef chuck roast (roasting joint)

• Kosher salt and freshly ground black pepper

• 4 tablespoons extra-virgin olive oil

• 2 large onions, halved through the root and thinly sliced

• 6 garlic cloves, thinly sliced

- 2 bay leaves

- 2 teaspoons onion powder

- 3⁄4 cup (175 ml/6 fl oz) dry red wine

- 1 cup (240 ml/8 fl oz) beef stock

- 1 can (28 oz/795 g) whole peeled tomatoes

- 1 lb (455 g) new potatoes, halved if large

- 2 large carrots, halved lengthwise if thick and cut crosswise into 2-inch (5 cm) pieces

Directions

- Preheat the oven to 325°F (160°C/Gas Mark 3).

- Season both sides of the roast with salt and pepper. In a Dutch oven (casserole) or other large ovenproof pot with a lid, heat 2 tablespoons of the oil over medium-high heat.

- Add the roast and sear, turning once, until browned on both sides, 8–10 minutes total.

- Remove the seared roast and set aside. Add the remaining

- 2 tablespoons oil to the pan followed by the onions, garlic, and bay leaves and cook, stirring often, until the onions soften, about 10 minutes. Add the onion powder and cook, stirring, until fragrant, about 1 minute.

• Add the wine, stock, tomatoes with their juice, and 1½ teaspoons salt. Gently break up the tomatoes with the back of a spoon and bring the mixture to a boil. Nestle the seared meat into the sauce, spooning an ample amount of sauce on top.

• Cover, transfer to the oven, and cook for 2 hours. Remove from the oven, uncover, and carefully flip the meat over.

• Add the potatoes and carrots, tucking them into the sauce. Re-cover and continue cooking until the vegetables are soft and meat is fork-tender, about 2 hours more.

• Transfer the meat to a carving board, drape loosely with foil, and let rest 10–15 minutes before slicing. Arrange the sliced meat on a serving platter and arrange the potatoes, carrots, and any larger tomato pieces around it. Discard the bay leaves. Set the pan over medium-high heat and boil, stirring occasionally, until reduced by one-third, about 10 minutes. Spoon the sauce over meat and vegetables and serve hot.

Mofelta

Ingredients

• 1 packet (1⁄4 oz/7 g) active dry yeast (2 1⁄4 teaspoons)

• 1 tablespoon sugar

• 1 1⁄2 cups (355 ml/12 fl oz) warm water (110°F/43°C)

• 4 cups (560 g) all-purpose (plain) flour, or more as needed

• 1 1⁄2 teaspoons kosher salt

• Vegetable oil, for greasing bowl, dough, and frying

Optional toppings:

• Salted butter, honey, jam, or finely chopped pistachios

Directions

• In a large bowl, stir together the yeast, sugar, and warm water. Let sit until foaming, 5–10 minutes.

• Meanwhile, in a medium bowl, whisk together the flour and salt.

• Add the flour mixture to the yeast mixture and stir until the dough begins to come together. Turn the dough out onto a lightly floured surface and knead well, adding a little additional flour, if needed, 1 tablespoon at a time, until you have a supple, slightly tacky dough, 5–10 minutes. (The kneading can also be done in a stand mixer with a dough hook, 5–7 minutes.) Grease a large bowl with about 1 teaspoon oil, add the dough, and turn to coat. Cover the bowl with a tea towel and let sit in a warm place until almost doubled in size, about 1 hour.

• Drizzle a large sheet pan with enough oil to coat the bottom. Pinch off a golf ball–size pieces of dough and roll into balls. Place the balls on the baking sheet, turning to coat in the oil, and let rest for 30 minutes.

• In a large nonstick frying pan, heat a few teaspoons oil over medium-low heat. While the oil is heating, take one of the dough balls and press it with your fingertips into a very thin round 8–10 inches (20–15 cm) in diameter.

• (It should be translucent, and it is okay if the dough tears a little.) Gently transfer the dough round to the frying pan and cook, flipping once, until golden brown on both sides, about 1 minute per side. Transfer to a plate.

• While the first dough round is frying, flatten the next one.

• Continue flattening and frying dough rounds in this manner, nudging the heat up or down as needed to avoid burning, until all of the dough balls are fried. As you work, layer the completed crepes on top of one another in a stack.

• Serve hot or warm with desired toppings.

Cinnamon–Golden Raisin Babka

Ingredients

For The Syrup:

• 1⁄2 cup (120 ml/4 fl oz) water

• 1⁄2 cup (100 g) granulated sugar

For The Dough:

• 1 packet (1⁄4 oz/7g) active dry yeast (21⁄4 teaspoons)

• 1⁄2 cup (100 g) plus 1 teaspoon sugar

• 1 cup (240 ml/8 fl oz) warm water (110°F/43°C)

• 4–5 cups (560–700 g) all-purpose (plain) flour

• 1 teaspoon kosher salt

• 2 eggs, lightly beaten

• 1 stick (4 oz/115 g) unsalted butter, cut into pieces, at room temperature

• 1 teaspoon vegetable oil

For The Filling:

• 1 cup (105 g) walnut halves

• 1 stick (4 oz/115 g) unsalted butter, cut into pieces, at room temperature

• 1 cup (200 g) sugar

• 2 teaspoons ground cinnamon

• 1 teaspoon vanilla extract

• 1 teaspoon finely grated orange zest

• 1 cup (140 g) golden raisins (sultanas)

Make The Syrup:

• In a small saucepan, bring the water and sugar to a boil over medium heat, stirring often to dissolve the sugar.

• Reduce the heat to medium-low and cook until the syrup thickens slightly, 3–5 minutes. Remove from the heat and let cool completely. Set aside until needed, or cover and refrigerate for up to 2 weeks.

Make The Dough:

• In a large bowl, stir together the yeast, 1 teaspoon sugar, and the warm water. Let sit until foaming, 5–10 minutes.

• Meanwhile, in a large bowl, whisk together 4 cups (560 g) flour and the salt.

• Stir the remaining ½ cup (100 g) sugar and the eggs into the yeast mixture. Add the flour mixture and gently stir until a wet dough comes together. Turn the dough out onto a floured surface and knead well, adding the softened butter pieces a few at a time, and adding up to 1 cup (140 g) additional flour as needed, until you have a supple, slightly tacky dough, about 10 minutes. You might not need all of the flour. (The kneading can also be done in a stand mixer with a dough hook, 5–7 minutes.)

• Grease a large bowl with the vegetable oil, add the dough, and turn to coat. Cover the bowl with plastic wrap (cling film) or a tea towel and let sit in a warm place until nearly doubled in size, 1–1 ½ hours.

Meanwhile, Make The Filling:

• In a food processor, combine the walnuts, butter, sugar, cinnamon, vanilla, and orange zest and pulse until a smooth paste forms.

• Grease three 9 × 5-inch (23 × 12.5 cm) loaf pans.

• Gently punch down the dough and turn out onto a lightly floured surface. Divide the dough into 3 equal portions.

• Working with one piece at a time (keep the rest covered in the bowl), roll out the dough into a large rectangle ¼ inch (6 mm) thick.

• Evenly spread about one-third of the filling onto dough, leaving a ¼-inch (6 mm) border around the edges. Evenly sprinkle one-third of the golden raisins (sultanas) on top.

• Starting at one of the short sides, roll the dough up tightly like a jelly roll (Swiss roll). Using a sharp knife, trim ½ inch

• (1.25 cm) off each end of the roll (and discard). Halve the roll lengthwise. You should now have 2 long strands of dough, with the layers of filling exposed. Twist the strands together and pinch at the top and bottom to seal.

• Carefully place into one of the prepared loaf pans. Repeat with the remaining pieces of dough and remaining filling and golden raisins. Loosely cover the pans with plastic wrap (cling film) or a tea towel and let rise for 30 minutes.

Ingredients

For the dough:

• 2 cups all-purpose flour

• 3/4 tsp salt

• 3 large eggs, beaten

• 3 Tbsp cold water, approximately

For the meat filling:

• 2 Tbsp vegetable oil

• 1 medium onion, chopped

• 1 medium clove garlic, finely chopped (optional)

• 3 cups chopped, cooked beef (about 12 ounces – can be either ground beef or finely chopped leftover brisket or roast)

- 1 large egg

- 1 tsp paprika

- salt and freshly ground black pepper to taste

- Chicken soup to serve

Directions

- To make the dough: Place the flour, salt and beaten eggs in a food processor. Process while gradually adding just enough water to have the dough form into a ball. Wrap the dough in plastic wrap and let rest for at least one hour.

- To make the filling: Heat the vegetable oil in a sauté pan over medium heat. Add the onion and garlic and cook, stirring frequently, for about 2-3 minutes, or until the vegetables have softened. Place the chopped meat in a bowl. Add the softened onion (and garlic), egg, paprika and salt and pepper to taste. Mix thoroughly.

- Roll the dough, a portion at a time, on a floured surface until the dough is very thin (less than 1/8-inch). Cut dough into 2-1/2 to 3-inch squares.

• Place one heaping teaspoon of filling in the center of each square. Fold the dough over the filling to make a triangle. Pinch the dough together to seal the edges (if necessary wet two sides of the square).

• Bring a large soup pot of water to a boil. Cook the kreplach about a dozen at a time for about 15 minutes, or until they are tender.

• To serve, place the cooked kreplach in chicken soup and cook for 4-5 minutes. You may also fry the kreplach in vegetable oil.

Baklava with Honey and Cardamom
Ingredients

• 16 oz. raw pistachios, walnuts, blanched almonds, or hazelnuts (or a mix, like 8 oz. raw pistachios and 8 oz. raw walnuts)

• 2 tsp cinnamon, ground

• 2 tsp cardamom, ground

• 1/4 cup honey or brown sugar

• 1 pack frozen phyllo dough sheets, thawed

- 1 cup oil (coconut or olive oil work well) or melted butter

Syrup:

- 1 1/2 cup honey

- 3/4 cup water

- 2 tbsp lemon juice

- Rind of 1 lemon, peeled

- Cinnamon stick

- 5 cardamom pods

- 2 Tbsp rose water

Directions

- Preheat oven to 350 degrees.

- First, add the nuts to a food processor. Pulse until the nuts are chopped finely but not ground into powder. Transfer to a bowl, and add cinnamon, cardamom and honey. Stir to combine.

- Next, prepare the dough. Gently take the roll of phyllo dough out from its package, taking care not to rip or tear the sheets. Unroll the dough and place a damp tea towel or paper towel over the top sheet to keep the dough from becoming dry and flaky.

• Place your bowl of melted butter or oil and the bowl of chopped nuts next to the stack of phyllo dough. Place your baking pan (9 inches x 12 inches x 2 inches) nearby.

• Using a pastry brush, oil the bottom and sides of the pan. Then carefully remove the top sheet of phyllo dough and place it in the pan. Lightly brush oil over the entire top of this sheet. Place another sheet of phyllo dough on top of the first sheet, brush oil on top, and add another sheet. Continue layering phyllo dough and oil until you have a stack of 10 sheets.

Sephardic Jeweled Rosh Hashanah Rice

Ingredients

• 1 1/2 tsp salt

• 1 tsp sweet paprika

• 1/2 tsp turmeric

• 1/4 tsp cumin

• 1/8 tsp black pepper

• 4 Tbsp extra virgin olive oil divided, plus 1 teaspoon

• 2 medium size onions, diced small

• 10 dried apricots, quartered

• 6 dried figs (we used Smyrna), quartered

• 1/4 cup dried cherries

• 1/4 cups pistachios or pumpkin seeds

• 1 cup long grain rice (we used Jasmine, but you can use Basmati or whatever you prefer)

• 1 cup water

• 1 1/2 tsp fresh lemon or orange zest

• 1 cup pomegranate seeds

Directions

• Combine salt, sweet paprika, turmeric, cumin and black pepper in a small bowl. Set aside.

• Heat 2 tablespoons of olive oil in a deep, non stick skillet with a lid. Add rice and spices and stir well.

• Cook over medium heat for about 3-4 minutes, stirring constantly and making sure the rice gets well coated with the oil and the spices.

• Add 1 cup of water. Bring to a boil, cover and reduce heat to low. Cook for 20 minutes, remove from heat and let it sit for 15 minutes covered.

• In the meantime, heat the remaining 2 tablespoons of olive oil in a non stick skillet.

• Add onions and cook over medium heat for about 20 minutes stirring frequently, adding water 1 tablespoon at a time if necessary, to prevent from burning.

• Transfer onions to a plate and in the same skillet, heat 1 teaspoon of olive oil. Add dried fruit and pistachios or pumpkin seeds and cook over medium low for 2-3 minutes, stirring frequently.

• Once the rice is ready, fluff it with a fork, add onions, dried fruit, pistachios and lemon or orange zest and toss well.

• Right before serving sprinkle pomegranate seeds on the rice.

Ingredients

For The Spice Rub:

• ¼ Cup sumac

• Zest from 1 lemon

• 1 tsp salt

• ¼ tsp white pepper (black pepper is fine too)

• 6 pieces bone-in, skin-on chicken legs (drumstick & thigh) or chicken breast

• 3 cups basmati or jasmine rice

• ½ cup pine nuts

• 3 tbsp berberis, dried cranberries or cherries

• 1 tsp turmeric

• ½ tsp salt

• 2 tbsp olive oil

• 1 red onion, cut in ½ inch thick slices

• 1 lemon, cut in 1/4 inch round slices

• 4 ½ cups (32 fl oz) chicken stock

• Olive oil

Directions

• Pre-heat the oven to 400°F with the rack in the middle.

• Make the spice rub by combining the sumac, lemon zest, salt and white pepper in a small bowl.

• Rub the spice mix under the skin and on top of the pieces of chicken.

• In a roasting pan, combine the rice, pine nuts, berberis, turmeric, salt and 2 tablespoons of olive oil until the rice is a beautiful yellow color. Press the rice down so it's pretty flat.

• Top the rice with the slices of red onion and lay the chicken pieces on top of the onions. Top each piece of chicken with a lemon slice.

• If you are assembling ahead of time and roasting later, this is the point you will want to cover the roasting pan with tin foil or lid and set in the fridge.

• Pour the stock around the chicken onto the rice. Drizzle the chicken with a decent amount of olive oil.

• Cover the roasting pan tightly with tin foil and place it in the oven. Roast for 40 minutes. Remove the foil and continue roasting for an additional 20-25 minutes until the chicken is cooked through and the rice has soaked up all of the liquids.

Stuffed Grape Leaves

Ingredients

• Juice of 2 lemons

• Lemon wedges

• Plain yogurt

• 1 cup olive oil

• 36-40 brine-packed grape leaves, well rinsed and patted dry

• 1/4 cup dried currants, plumped in hot water until softened and drained

• 1/4 cup pine nuts, toasted (optional)

• 2 teaspoons salt

- 1 teaspoon freshly ground black pepper

- 6 tablespoons chopped fresh mint

- 1/4 cup chopped fresh flat-leaf parsley

- 1/4 cup finely chopped fresh fennel leaves

- 2/3 cup peeled, seeded, and diced tomato

- 1 cup long-grain white rice, soaked in water for 30 minutes and draine

- 3 tablespoons olive oil

- 2 onion, chopped

- 3 cloves garlic, smashed

Directions

- To make the filling, warm the olive oil in a sautee pan over medium heat. Add the onions and sautee until tender and translucent, about 10 minutes. Add the garlic and sautee for a few minutes longer. Add the drained rice to the sautee pan along with all of the remaining ingredients. Stir well and remove from the heat.

• Lay out some of the grape leaves on a work surface, shiny side down. Snip off the stems with scissors. Place a teaspoon or so of the mixture near the stem end of a leaf. Fold the stem end over the filling, fold in the sides, and then roll up the leaf into a cylinder. Do not roll too tightly, as the rice expands during cooking. Repeat until all the filling is used.

• Place the filled leaves, close to each other and seam side down, in a single layer in a wide saucepan. Pour the olive oil, lemon juice, and hot water to cover over them. Place 1 or 2 heavy plates only slightly smaller than the diameter of the pan on top of the leaves to weight them down. Make sure that the leaves are just covered with liquid, adding more hot water, if necessary.

• Bring the liquids to a boil over medium heat, cover, reduce the heat to low, and simmer gently until the filling is cooked, 35 to 40 minutes. Remove from the heat, uncover, and remove the plate(s) so that the stuffed leaves can cool quickly.

• Using a spatula, transfer the filled leaves to a platter. Cool to room temperature before serving. (They can be transferred to a container, covered, and refrigerated for up to 1 week; bring to room temperature before serving.) Accompany with lemon wedges and a bowl of yogurt.

Ingredients

• 1/2 cup orange juice

• 1 cup dried apricots, prunes, or a combination of any dried fruit

• 12 cloves garlic, minced

• 1/2-inch piece fresh ginger, peeled and finely chopped (about 1 1/2 Tbsp)

• 2 Tbsp dried oregano

• 1 Tbsp dried thyme

• 1/3 cup red wine vinegar

• 3 Tbsp extra-virgin olive oil

• 1 1/2 Tbsp fresh lemon juice

• 2 bay leaves

• 2 (3- to 4-pound) chickens, cut into 8 pieces

- 1 1/2 tsp kosher salt

- 1/2 tsp ground black pepper

- 1/2 cup packed light brown sugar

- 1/2 cup white wine

Directions

- In a small bowl, pour orange juice over dried fruit and let soak to plump the fruit, about 10 minutes. In a separate small bowl, whisk together garlic, ginger, oregano, thyme, vinegar, olive oil, lemon juice, and bay leaves.

- Place chickens in two roasting pans. Pour marinade equally over each chicken and massage into chicken. Add orange juice and fruit mixture equally to each roasting pan.

- Cover pans and marinate in the refrigerator for 4 hours or overnight.

- Preheat oven to 375°F. Sprinkle chicken with salt and pepper, and then drizzle equally with brown sugar and white wine. Bake until chicken is nicely browned on top and registers 165°F in the thickest part of the thigh, about 1 hour and 15 minutes.

• Serve with pan juices and dried fruit.

Ingredients

For the court bouillon (cooking broth):

• 4 quarts water

• ½ bunch fresh thyme

• ½ bunch fresh flat leaf parsley

• ¼ tsp whole black peppercorns

• ¼ tsp whole fennel seeds

• 2 ½ cups dry white wine

• 1 medium onion, thinly sliced

• 1 medium carrot, peeled and sliced into ¼-inch rounds

• ½ lemon, cut into ¼-inch slices

• 2 bay leaves

• 1 Tbsp coarse salt

For The Fish:

• 1½ pounds skinless filleted halibut

- 1½ pounds skinless filleted salmon

- 2 medium onions, grated (about 1 cup)

- 2 medium carrots, peeled and finely grated (about ½ cup)

- Finely grated zest of 1 organic lemon

- 1 Tbsp minced celery or minced fennel fronds

- 3 extra-large eggs

- 6 Tbsp matzah meal

- 6 Tbsp water

- 1 to 3 tablespoons sugar

- 1½ Tbsp kosher salt

- 1 tsp freshly ground black pepper

Directions

• For the court bouillon (cooking broth), fill a stockpot with the water. Place the thyme, parsley, peppercorns and fennel seeds in a small piece of cheesecloth, knot to enclose, and add to the stockpot. Add the wine, onion, carrot, lemon, bay leaves and salt.

• Cover the pot and bring to a simmer over medium-low heat. Remove the lid, and simmer gently for 30 minutes. Remove and discard the cheesecloth package.

• For the fish, cut the fillets into 1-inch pieces. Working in batches, pulse the fish in a food processor until roughly ground.

• Place the ground fish in a large bowl and add the onions, carrots, zest, celery or fennel fronds, eggs, matzah meal, water, sugar (to taste), salt and pepper. Mix until just combined. Chill in the refrigerator for 30 minutes.

• Fill a medium bowl with ice water. Wetting your hands in the water as you work, form ½-cup portions (3 to 4 ounces each) of the fish mixture into ovals or round balls. Bring the court bouillon to a gentle simmer.

• Add enough fish cakes to make one layer in the pot and poach until the fish turns opaque and its shape is set, about 3 minutes. Add the rest. Simmer, continuing to poach the fish until cooked through, 30 minutes.

• Remove the pan from the heat and allow the gefilte fish to cool in the bouillon, about 20 minutes.

• Remove the fish from the bouillon and transfer to a storage container. Ladle 2 tablespoons of the bouillon over the fish, cover the container and chill.

• Serve with your favorite horseradish.

Meatballs

Ingredients

• 2 cups walnuts

• 2 cups shitake mushrooms

• 2 cloves garlic

• 1⁄2 cup onion (chopped)

• 1 teaspoon thyme

• 1⁄2 teaspoon salt

• 1⁄2 cup matzo meal

• oil (for frying)

Directions

• Process mushrooms, walnuts, garlic and onion in a blender

- Add spices and matzo meal and mix thoroughly

- Heat oil in a frying pan

- Roll into small meatballs and fry in oil until all sides are browned

- Serve warm

Almost Instant Chocolate Pudding

Ingredients

- 1/2 cup granulated sugar

- 1/4 cup cornstarch

- 1/4 cup cocoa powder (Dutch-process is ideal)

- 1/4 teaspoon sea salt, fine

- 1 5/8 cup non-dairy vanilla milk (soy, almond or coconut)

- 1 1/2 ounce dark chocolate, 59-62% (chopped into small pieces)

- 1 teaspoon vanilla extract

Directions

Make a double portion of this recipe for the Brooklyn Blackout Cake.

• Sift the sugar, cornstarch, cocoa powder, and salt through a wire mesh strainer into a medium saucepan. Slowly stir in the milk. Keep stirring until no trace of any of the dry ingredients is visible. The idea is to make sure the cornstarch is completely dissolved before you turn on the heat.

• Cook over medium-high heat, whisking frequently, until the mixture begins to thicken and is close to a boil. This can take as long as 12 minutes. Adjust the heat as needed to get a full boil, but don't let it be so high that the bottom scorches. As soon as the pudding starts to boil, it will thicken to pudding consistency. Immediately lower the heat and boil gently for another minute, stirring frequently with a silicone spatula.

• Remove the saucepan from the heat. Gently stir in the chocolate with the silicone spatula until the chocolate is melted and incorporated. Stir in the vanilla.

• Spoon the pudding into a bowl. It will be set and ready to use in about 30 minutes at room temperature, but it can be refrigerated for up to 24 hours. If you refrigerate it, cover the surface with plastic wrap, making sure the wrap adheres to the pudding to prevent a skin from forming.

Ingredients

• 3 very ripe bananas (mashed)

• 1 tablespoon fresh squeezed lemon juice

• 1/2 cup almond oil (you can use canola oil instead if you're in a pinch)

• 1/2 cup sweetner

• 3/4 cups chopped dates or raisins (if desired)

• 1 1/2 cup flour (preferably unbleached or whole wheat)

• 1/2 cup wheat germ

• 1/2 teaspoon sea salt

• 1/2 teaspoon baking powder

• 1/2 teaspoon baking soda

Directions

• Preheat oven to 375 degrees. In a small bowl, mash the bananas with a fork or a potato masher until very mushy, then add the lemon juice, oil, sweetener, and dates or raisins and stir together. In a separate large bowl, stir together the flour, wheat germ, sea salt, baking powder, and baking soda. Add the banana mixture to the flour mixture and mix together gently until "just mixed" (this is important! do NOT over mix! or the bread will be heavy when baked and not light, fluffy, and moist). The batter will seem thick, but it's supposed to be thick! It won't be 'thick' once it's baked. Spoon into a lightly oiled loaf pan and bake 40-50 minutes (usually takes about 40 minutes in my oven). Test with a knife to see if done.

Bbaba Waffles

Ingredients

- 1 banana

- 1 cup water

- 1 cup soy milk

- 1 teaspoon vanilla extract

- 1 1/2 cup flour

- 1/2 cup rolled oat flakes

- 2 teaspoons baking powder

- 1 teaspoon cinnamon

- 1/2 teaspoon nutmeg (optional)

Directions

- In a food processor, blend the banana and water until smooth. Add remaining ingredients and blend until well combined. Spoon into a well oiled, hot waffle iron. Repeat until batter is gone. Makes 4-8 waffles depending on the size of your waffle iron.

Beet Linguine with Cashew Ricotta

Ingredients

- 1 large head of garlic

- 4 teaspoons olive oil (divided)

- 2 cups raw cashews (soaked for 2-4 hours)

- 4 teaspoons nutritional yeast

- 2 tablespoons fresh lemon juice

- 1 teaspoon sea salt

- 5 teaspoons apple cider vinegar

- 1⁄2 pound beets (greens removed)

- 1 1⁄2 tablespoon olive oil (divided)

- 1 medium red onion (chopped, 1 1/2 cups)

- 1⁄2 teaspoon balsamic vinegar

- 1⁄2 teaspoon mirin (rice wine)

- 8 ounces whole wheat linguine

- 1⁄4 cup chopped flat-leaf parsley

Directions

- To make Cashew Ricotta: Preheat oven to 400°F. Slice off top of garlic head, drizzle with 1 tsp. oil, and wrap in parchment paper, then in foil. Roast 1 hour, or until soft.

- Rinse and drain soaked cashews, and transfer to food processor. Add remaining 1 Tbs. oil, nutritional yeast, lemon juice, salt, and vinegar. Squeeze roasted garlic from cloves into food processor, and blend until smooth. Transfer to medium bowl.

• To make Linguine: Bring beets and enough water to cover by 1 inch to a boil in large saucepan. Cover, reduce heat to medium-low, and simmer 35 to 40 minutes, or until beets are tender. Drain beets, and slip off skins under cool running water. Coarsely chop beets, and set aside.

• Heat 1 Tbs. oil in large skillet over medium heat. Add onion, and sauté 8 to 10 minutes. Reduce heat to medium-low, and cook 15 minutes more. Stir in balsamic vinegar and mirin. Cook 2 minutes, or until liquid evaporates. Transfer onion mixture to food processor, add beets, and purée until smooth. Season with salt and pepper, if desired, and transfer to medium saucepan. Keep warm.

• Cook pasta according to package directions. Drain, reserving 3 Tbs. pasta water. Return pasta to pot; toss with beet sauce, remaining 1 1/2 tsp. oil, and reserved pasta water. Top each serving with 2 Tbs. Cashew Ricotta, and sprinkle with chopped parsley.

Blueberry Blintzes

Ingredients

• 1 cup white spelt flour

• 1/8 teaspoon sea salt

- 2 tablespoons sugar

- 1/4 teaspoon baking soda

- 1 cup soy milk

- 1/4 cup water

- 2 tablespoons vegan butter

- 1/2 teaspoon freshly squeezed lemon juice or apple cider vinegar

- 1/2 teaspoon vanilla extract

- oil for the crepes

- 7 ounces extra firm tofu

- 8 ounces vegan cream cheese

- 2 tablespoons nutritional yeast

- 2 tablespoons tahini

- 1 tablespoon freshly squeezed lemon juice

- 1/4 cup organic sugar

- 1/4 teaspoon sea salt

- 8 ounces frozen or fresh blueberries

- 1/2 cup water (add 1/4 cup more water if fresh blueberries)

- 2 tablespoons organic sugar (or to taste)

- 1/8 teaspoon ground cardamom

- 1 tablespoon arrowroot powder dissolved in 2 tablespoons cold water

Directions

- Prepare the crepes and stack them on a plate:

- Place the dry ingredients in a bowl and whisk well. Place the wet ingredients in another bowl and mix well. Add the wet to the dry and mix well.

- Place a crepe pan over high heat and lightly oil. Pour a rounded 1/4 cup of batter onto the pan and spread as thinly as possible. Cook until bubbles form over the entire surface, approximately 3 minutes, depending on the heat of the pan. Carefully flip and cook for an additional 3 minutes. Repeat until all of the batter is used. Mix the batter in between crepes to maintain a uniform consistency.

• Prepare the filling by placing a pot with 1 inch of water and a steamer basket on high heat. Place the tofu in the steamer basket, cover and cook for 5 minutes. Remove the tofu and rinse well under cold water.

• Meanwhile, place the remaining filling ingredients in a bowl and mix well. Crumble the tofu into the bowl with the filling ingredients and mix well.

• Prepare the sauce by placing all of the ingredients, except the arrowroot mixture, in a small pot over medium heat and stir well. Cook for 5 minutes, stirring occasionally. Add the arrowroot mixture, reduce the heat to low, and stir well. Cook over low heat until the blintzes are finished cooking, stirring occasionally.

• To prepare the blintzes, place approximately 1/4 cup of the filling in the center of each crepe, towards the bottom. Fold in the sides, and then roll the crepe away from you, pulling the bottom portion towards you to create a tight wrap. Repeat with the remaining crepes and reserve approximately 1/2 cup of the filling to garnish the blintze.

• Heat oil in a large sauté pan. Place the blintzes in the pan and cook for 3 minutes on each side. Serve warm topped with confectioner's sugar if using, a liberal amount of sauce, and a dollop of the filling. Garnish with mint leaves if using.

Borscht

Ingredients

• 3 tablespoons olive oil

• 1 onion, large (chopped)

• 6 cloves garlic (smashed)

• 3 bay leaves

• 3 carrots (sliced)

• 8 beets, large (diced or julienne)

• 1 cabbage (shredded or thinly sliced)

• 28 ounces can of diced or crushed tomatoes (in juice, not puree)

• 1/4 teaspoon basil, dried

• 1/2 teaspoon celery seed

• 1 bunch parsley, chopped and fresh

• 1 bunch dill, chopped

• 2 lemons, juice only

Directions

• Prepare vegetables as specified above.

• In a large pot or soup kettle, sauté the onions, whole garlic and bay leaves in olive oil on low heat, stirring periodically, until quite tender, 20-30 minutes.

• Add carrots and beets and sauté another 5-10 minutes.

• Add the cabbage and stir. Then add tomatoes, basil, celery seed and water. How much water? Enough to cover.

• Cook at a gentle simmer for 1-2 hours.

• Add parsley and dill. Taste. Add salt, pepper, more celery seed if needed, and lemon juice to taste. Add water if soup needs thinning.

Brisket
Ingredients

• 2 cans crushed tomatoes (28 oz)

• 1/4 cup brown sugar

- 2 tablespoons agave/maple syrup

- 1/4 cup apple cider vinegar

- 1/2 cup water

- 1/2 cup red wine ((can also use grape juice or sweet kosher wine like Manischewitz))

- 1 onion (chopped)

- 3 cloves garlic (minced, grated, or pressed)

- 2 cans jackfruit (drained)

Directions

- Combine crushed tomatoes, brown sugar, apple cider vinegar, water, wine, onion and garlic in a large pot over medium-high heat. Bring to a boil then add jackfruit.

- Reduce heat to low-medium and cover pot.

- Cook for 30 minutes over low-medium heat.

- Remove cover and test whether you can break up the jackfruit using the back of a wooden spoon. If the jackfruit isn't tender enough to pull yet, cook it for another 15-20 minutes, or until tender.

- Serve warm.

Ingredients

- 3 cups butternut squash

- 1 tablespoon olive oil

- 1 red onion (thinly sliced)

- 2 cloves garlic (minced)

- 1 teaspoon cumin

- 1/2 teaspoon coriander, dried

- 1/4 teaspoon cinnamon

- 1 cup couscous, dried

- 1 cup cashews, raw

- 1/2 cup raisans

- 2 tablespoons lemon juice

- 1 ounce cilantro, fresh

Directions

• Preheat oven to 390°F and line a tray with parchment/baking paper. Chop and dice the butternut squash into 1-inch cubes. Place the diced squash onto the baking tray and drizzle with a little bit of olive oil. Season with salt and pepper. Bake for 35 to 40 minutes until lightly browned.

• Cook couscous according to package instructions. Set aside. In a fry pan on high heat, add the 1 tablespoon of olive oil or spray the pan with oil. Add the onion to the fry pan and sauté until transparent. Add the garlic and sauté until fragrant. Add the cumin, dried coriander, cinnamon, roasted squash and cashews. Sauté for a couple of minutes until heated through while softly breaking the pumpkin up with your spatula. Add in the cooked couscous, raisins, lemon juice and season with salt and pepper. Sauté for another minute or so until heated through and the spices have been evenly distributed.

• Take the fry pan off the heat and throw in the cilantro. Toss to combine. Serve immediately with lemon wedges.

Cake Brooklyn Blackout

Ingredients

- 2 cups granulated sugar

- 1 1⁄2 cup pastry flour, whole wheat

- 1 1⁄2 cup all-purpose flour

- 2⁄3 cups cocoa powder, natural

- 2 teaspoons baking soda

- 1 teaspoon sea salt, fine

- 2 cups water (room temperature)

- 2⁄3 cups olive oil, extra virgin (mild-tasting)

- 3 tablespoons maple syrup

- 2 tablespoons apple cider vinegar

- 1 tablespoon vanilla extract, pure

- 1 teaspoon chocolate extract (optional)

Directions

- Position a rack in the middle of the oven and preheat to 350° F. Oil the sides and bottoms of two 9 x 3-inch round cake pans. Line the bottoms with parchment circles. Do not oil the paper.

• Place a wire mesh strainer over a large bowl. Add the sugar, whole wheat pastry flour, all-purpose flour, cocoa, baking soda, and salt to the strainer and stir with a wire whisk to sift the ingredients into the bowl. (If any small bits remain in the strainer, add them to the mixture in the bowl.) Whisk to aerate the mixture.

• Whisk the water, oil, maple syrup, vinegar, vanilla, and chocolate extract (if using) in a separate medium bowl until completely combined. Immediately pour into the dry mixture and whisk until the batter is smooth.

• Divide the batter between the 2 pans. Rotate the pans to level the batter and tap them lightly on the counter to eliminate air bubbles.

• Bake on the middle rack for 30 to 35 minutes, or until the tops of the cakes are set, the sides have started to pull away from the pan, and a wooden toothpick or skewer inserted into the center comes out clean or with just a few moist crumbs.

• Set the cakes on wire racks. After 5 minutes, run a thin knife around the sides of each cake to release the sides of the cake from the pan. Invert each cake onto a rack.

Remove the pans and carefully peel off the parchment paper. It is fine to cool the cakes bottom side up.

• When the cakes are completely cool, slide a 9-inch cardboard cake circle under each one. Wrap the layers with plastic wrap and refrigerate for about 1 hour, or until cold.

• Use a long serrated knife to slice each cake layer in half horizontally to form four layers. Crumble one of the layers into a food processor. Pulse the processor a few times to make medium-size crumbs, but stop before they get too fine. Pour the crumbs into a bowl.

• 9. Line a rimmed baking sheet with parchment paper. Place one of the remaining three layers, still on the cake circle, on the baking sheet. Spread with a scant cup of the pudding. Place a second cake layer on the pudding, board side up. Remove the board and spread the layer with another scant cup of pudding. Slip the board under the last layer and invert it onto the cake. Spread with another scant cup of the pudding. Refrigerate the cake and remaining pudding for 20 minutes. (It is easier to finish a cold cake.)

• 10. Cover the sides of the cake with the remaining pudding. Sprinkle the top and sides of the cake liberally with the cake crumbs, completely covering the pudding. Pat the crumbs lightly to make sure they adhere. Use all the crumbs, even the ones that fall onto the paper

Ingredients

• 2 large russet potatoes, grated or spiralized

• 1 medium onion, sliced thinly

• 2 cloves garlic, minced

• 1 teaspoon paprika

• 1 tablespoon cornstarch

• Salt, to taste

Direction

• Preheat oven to 400°F and spray a muffin pan with non-stick spray.

• In the meantime, sauté your onion and garlic over medium-high heat until they appear soft and translucent.

• Add sautéed onions and garlic and potato to large mixing bowl, and stir to combine.

• Add salt, paprika, and cornstarch to the mixing bowl, and stir until veggies are evenly coated.

• Push mixture into muffin pan, filling each space to the top, and bake for 40 minutes.

Latkes With Fennel and Avocado Tartare

Ingredients

For the Latkes:

• 3 potatoes

• 1 onion

• Salt, to taste

• Black pepper, freshly ground

• Neutral-tasting vegetable oil, for frying

For the Tartare:

• Fennel

• 1/2 cucumber

• Green apple

• 1 avocado, halved

• 3 tablespoons fresh lemon juice

• 1/4 teaspoon salt

• Black pepper, freshly ground

• Prepared horseradish or freshly grated horseradish, to taste

• Bundle of fresh dill

• Capers (optional)

Direction

To Make the Latkes:

• Grate potatoes and onion coarsely. Put grated vegetables to bowl and season with salt. Gather mixture inside kitchen towel and squeeze out as much liquid as possible. Set mixture into a sieve and let it drain. While they drain, make the tartare.

• Heat a splash of oil on a skillet. Cover the bottom of a smaller skillet or heavy pot with kitchen foil. Season the potato mixture with black pepper.Test temperature of the skillet with potato strip: if oil starts to sizzle it's hot enough.

• Drop small amounts (about 2 tablespoons) of potato mixture to a pan and press them down with the back of the spoon.

• Place the foil-covered skillet on top of the latkes and fry them over medium-high heat for a couple of minutes (until golden brown). Flip latkes and cover them again with the skillet. Continue frying for another couple of minutes.

• Line a big plate with a coffee filter or kitchen paper towels. Set latkes on the plate when they are done. Repeat with the rest of the potato mixture. Add more oil between batches when necessary. Serve immediately with fennel and avocado tartare

To Make the Tartare:

• Cut fennel half lengthwise. Separate stalks and remove hard stem. Cut both fennel halves to four and slice each part finely. Cut the stalks half and slice them into thin half moons. Cut cucumber and apple to small dices. Half the avocado.

• Purée one half of the avocado and lemon juice with an immersion blender (or smash it with a fork). Season avocado mixture with salt, pepper and horseradish.

Combine vegetables and avocado dressing. Dice remaining half of the avocado and chop dill finely. Mix avocado and minced dill (and capers) with rest of the salad

Ingredients

• Crust

• ½ cup hazelnuts

• ½ cup ground almonds

• ½ cup soaked dates chopped

• 1 tsp almond extract

Cherry Cheesecake layer

• 1 ½ cup pitted fresh cherries

• ½ cup soaked cashews

• ¼ cup agave nectar

• 1 tbsp coconut oil

• 1 tbsp lemon juice

Vanilla Cheesecake layer

- 1 ½ cups soaked cashews

- ½ cup agave nectar

- 1 tsp vanilla extract

- Juice ½ lemon

- ¼ cup filtered water

  Topping

  ½ cup flaked almonds

Direction

- Place the cashews in a large bowl and cover with filtered water. Allow to stand for 4-6hrs. Soak the dates in a smaller bowl for about an hour or until they are reasonably soft. Otherwise you could just use medjool dates, which are already very soft.

- Place all the crust ingredients into a food processor or blender and blend until crumbly. Line a cake tin with baking parchment and turn the crust mixture into it. Press firmly to the edges using the back of your fingers. Place in freezer for 30 mins.

• Rinse out the blender and add the cherries, agave and lemon juice. Blitz until completely smooth, it should be liquid like. Next add the cashews and coconut oil and blitz until completely smooth and creamy. It should be quite thick. Taste for sweetness, if you prefer it sweeter then add a little more agave.

• Take the crust out of the freezer and carefully pour in the cherry cheesecake mixture, scraping down the sides with a spatula (waste not, want not!). Smooth with a spatula until it is completely even and return to freezer for an hour.

• Meanwhile, rinse out the blender again and add all the ingredients for the vanilla layer. Blitz until completely smooth. This layer will be less thick and almost more like a cashew cream. When the cherry layer has set carefully pour over the vanilla mixture. Smooth with a spatula, sprinkle over the flaked almonds and place in the freezer for several hours.

• When it has set, transfer to the fridge for 30mins before trying to remove it from the tin.